SHAD HELMSTETTER, PH.D.

Best-Selling Author of
What to Say When You Talk to Your Self

A 60-Minute Book™

SELF-TALK *for* SELF-ESTEEM

How Negative Self-Talk Wires Low Self-Esteem Into Your Brain—and How to Change It!

Self-Talk for Self-Esteem

By Shad Helmstetter, Ph.D.

Self-Talk for Self-Esteem

Published by Park Avenue Press
362 Gulf Breeze Pkwy., #104
Gulf Breeze, FL 32561

Helmstetter, Shad
Self-Talk for Self-Esteem

ISBN: 978-1-7344982-4-0 *Printed format*

Books by Shad Helmstetter

What to Say When You Talk to Your Self
The Power of Neuroplasticity
365 Days of Positive Self-Talk
Negative Self-Talk and How to Change It
The Secret Words of Success

Table of Contents

Chapter One

Your Self-Esteem

There are few changes you can make in your life that are more helpful than an upward change in your self-esteem.

Your self-esteem affects everything about you and everything you do; there is nothing about you that *isn't* affected by how you see yourself. A strong, healthy self-esteem helps you look at life in a positive, believing way. It helps you deal with life and its problems—and come out on top.

The other kind of self-esteem—negative self-esteem—causes you to doubt yourself and your abilities. It gives you a false, diminished picture of yourself. It holds you back and allows life's challenges to overcome you. And perhaps worst of all, negative self-esteem causes you to live days and years of your life without ever liking yourself as much as you should, so it keeps you from getting to know the wonderful person you were born to be.

There is a direct link between your self-talk and your self-esteem—so much so, that it is no longer sufficient to discuss self-esteem without also discussing self-talk in the same conversation. In this book, we're going to discuss both your self-esteem and your self-talk, and find out how and why they are inextricably tied together throughout your life.

I've been researching, writing about, and conducting seminars on this subject for forty years. During that time, I've written more than twenty books. The first of these, *What to Say When You Talk to Your Self,* is published today in over 70 countries, which is a testament to how important the subjects of self-talk and self-esteem are to many people.

You could look at the book you're reading now as my personal notes for a seminar. It is a textbook of sorts; I have underlined the points which I believe are the most important, and kept commentary to a minimum. Throughout, it should be easy to read and understand.

In this book, we'll cover the basics of self-talk—what it is and how it works, the important science behind it, and how to apply what we have learned about self-talk to the goal of creating stronger, healthier self-esteem.

I have also included key information that I've written previously on this subject, so that, even without reading any of my other books, you can be sure you have the most complete picture possible.

If you're reading the printed version of this book, you'll notice it is printed in larger type, in an open format, with fewer pages than a standard, full-length book. That's because this book is written in a more accessible '60-Minute Book' format. This format is designed to give you as much information as possible in the shortest amount of time (about an hour or so of reading).

If You Want to Change Your Self-Esteem, You *Can*

During the many years I've been studying and writing about this subject, it has become crystal clear to me that anyone who wants to improve their self-esteem can do so. No matter where you've been in your life up to now, no matter how badly the world has treated you—or how badly you may have treated yourself—as long as you're still here and still breathing, you can improve your self-esteem.

Take heart. This is a battle you can win!

Chapter Two

The Real Meaning of Self-Esteem

It is popularly thought that self-esteem means "self-love." But that's not what it really means.

A more appropriate definition of self-esteem—and the definition we're using here—comes from its roots: Self-esteem means "self-estimation." (The word *esteem* is derived from the Latin 'aestimare' – to *estimate.*)

Your self-esteem is your estimation of who you believe yourself to be. It is your mental appraisal of you—the personal, wired-in *opinion* you have of everything about you.

When someone says, *"I have low self-esteem,"* what they're really saying is, *"I underestimate myself"* or, *"I have a problem with my opinion of myself."*

That's an accurate picture of what's really taking place—and it also gets right to the heart of the matter: Having low self-esteem is almost always the result of having an inaccurate opinion of yourself. Because of this, fixing your self-esteem is more about fixing your *opinion* of yourself than it is about fixing the self-imagined faults in your makeup.

To illustrate this, think of someone you know who has low self-esteem. Your opinion of that person is almost always higher than the opinion that person has of himself or herself. *You* can see their qualities, but they can't see them. So it isn't a lack of qualities that's the problem; it's the person's inability to see them. They have gotten into the habit of seeing their faults instead of their qualities.

Can You Have Too Much Self-Esteem?

Some people have argued that you can have too *much* self-esteem. People who take this position often refer to the idea of kids getting trophies for 'just showing up.' But their argument is based on two false premises.

The first is, they think self-esteem simply means 'self-love,' and they think that having too much of it creates a kind of narcissistic self-centeredness. But as we just saw, that's not what self-esteem means.

Their argument also assumes that self-esteem is taught in a vacuum, with no other positive qualities being developed along with it. So they believe, incorrectly, that 'praise' leads to a person being selfish or egotistical, unrealistic and unprepared to deal with life as it really is.

But that's not how the development of self-esteem works. An integral part of developing healthy self-esteem are the values that are part of positive self-esteem itself—values such as *taking personal responsibility for yourself, showing genuine compassion for others, making good choices, exercising self-discipline, using manners, being mindful,* and *having balance in all things.*

That's not having too much self-esteem—that's a quality human being.

You Are Not Your Self-Esteem

Unless your estimation of yourself is perfectly accurate (and it almost never is), *you are not your self-esteem, and your self-esteem is not you.* They only *seem* to be one and the same, but they're not.

There is the real, *true,* you as you actually are—and, in the case of low self-esteem, there is the negative, *usually inaccurate* picture of you that you imagine yourself to be. In fact, in all likelihood, your *estimation* of who you are may be very different from who you really are—or who you *can* be if you choose to be.

It is a fact of the makeup of the human mind that you become most how you describe yourself most. You live up to, or down to, the image you create of yourself in your mind. And what creates this picture of yourself that you carry in your mind? The number one source for the beliefs you carry about you is your self-talk.

So I'll start by bringing you up-to-date on self-talk itself, how it came to be as we know it today, and why it plays such an important role in your self-esteem.

Chapter Three

A Brief History of Self-Talk

Although the idea of self-talk is very old, recent discoveries in the field of neuroscience have led to a new understanding of self-talk and how it plays a key role in wiring our brains for success or failure.

My own interest in self-talk began after I had served as a foreign language interpreter for the United States government in Cuba during the Cuban Missile Crisis.

I was deeply interested in understanding how the human brain becomes programmed, and how our mental programs become imbedded in our brains. Because I had studied foreign languages, I recognized that mental programming was very much like learning a language—imprinting a vocabulary that both determines and expresses our thoughts, and ultimately structures our beliefs.

It was clear to me that our self-talk—the 'language' we think in and the actual vocabulary we use throughout each day—plays a significant role in determining not only how we think, but also how we see the world each day. The question I asked was, *"What if we could change how we see the world, and how we deal with life, by changing the language we use when we talk to ourselves?"*

The idea made sense. But as I began my research into how to reprogram the human brain for success in life, I had no idea how accurate that first assumption was: *we become most what we think most.*

At the time, in the general public, there seemed to be only a passing interest in the idea that our thoughts created our self-esteem, and that our self-esteem, in turn, determined our destinies. Writers in the self-help field, especially in the area of positive thinking, understood the basic concept of the power of thought, but neuroscience had not yet shown how it actually worked.

Meanwhile, convinced that the answer had to do with how our thoughts themselves were *physically* rewiring our brains, I continued to forge ahead, certain that self-talk was the mind/brain/success connection we had been looking for.

That recognition ultimately let to a choice to continue studying self-talk, which I have done for the past four decades. It was during this time that I came to recognize self-talk as one of the most significant developments ever uncovered in our understanding of human behavior.

It was because of my earlier experience with language training that, in the early 1980s, even before I wrote my first book on the subject, my initial step into the world of self-talk was to produce a series of recorded, self-talk audio programs that were designed to teach the listener a new 'language'—with a positive new vocabulary. (The method was similar to listening to language tapes when you wanted to learn a foreign language.)

This time, however, the new language would be a language that would focus on 'life success.' The recorded self-talk sessions were based on solid behavioral concepts that included personal responsibility, self-belief, setting goals, and taking positive action, and they were designed to help the listeners imprint clear, new—and more successful—thought patterns in their brains.

The idea worked extremely well, and the result was that, in a short time, there were people from every walk of life who were starting their day each morning by listening to recorded self-talk sessions that included subjects like weight loss, career improvement, and financial success. By listening to these early self-talk sessions every day, people were literally rewiring their brains with completely new mental programs—a new language of success.

What the early self-talk listeners proved was that, with only a small amount of effort, any individual could actually change *what* they thought, and *how* they thought—and the action they would take—as a result of the new 'language' they were learning.

I had started this research by using myself as my first test subject. At the time, I needed to lose a lot of weight, but, like so many people, I had failed at every diet I had tried. Because of my interest in self-talk, I came to the conclusion that my weight problem might actually be a problem of my overweight *thinking*. So I decided to change my self-talk. By listening to recordings of newly-worded, very healthy self-talk, in just over 10 weeks I lost 58 pounds! I was convinced. And to bring the point home, this time the weight didn't come back! (Now, years later, it still hasn't.)

As I continued to study the concept of self-talk and what it could do, I began to recognize that the role of self-talk in personal well-being was so vitality important that everyone should be made aware of it. I saw, even then, the potential impact that changing a person's self-talk could have on their life. I was also concerned that the concept of self-talk should be taken seriously, and not be tossed into the bin with 'wishful thinking' or short-term motivational enthusiasm.

I knew that, applied correctly, self-talk was *foundational*. Understanding it offered a deeper, and profoundly important, insight into how the human brain becomes programmed for success or for failure in anything.

Meanwhile, with new developments in brain imaging technology, science was beginning to support my conclusions. Research in the field of neuroscience was showing that repeated inputs to the brain were actually physically rewiring the structure of the brain itself—precisely the foundation on which self-talk is based.

To ensure that the new information on self-talk—and what it could do to help individual lives—would be made available to as many people as possible, in 1985 I founded the Self-Talk Institute. (It remains, to this day, the world's leading organization in the field of self-talk.) It is the objective of the Institute to study the science and application of self-talk techniques, and to make learning self-talk available to individuals worldwide.

To reach that goal, the Institute trains and certifies self-talk trainers who teach the message of self-talk to audiences throughout the United States and in other countries. The Institute also maintains a very popular website (www.selftalkplus.com), which continues to stream recorded self-talk audio sessions every day to listeners around the world.

The concept of self-talk has also become a major factor in how human behavior is understood in the academic world. Self-talk, and the wiring of the human brain, is now at the core of advancements in the fields of psychology, physiology, health, sports, and education. Self-talk—both the positive and the negative kind—is known to play a primary role in every facet of human development and expression.

The idea of managing or changing our self-talk has come of age. We now know that self-talk is playing a pivotal, directing role in every important area of our lives: our health, our relationships, our careers, our income, our well-being—and most significantly, in forming our *self-esteem.*

And it is where self-esteem is formed, that our future begins.

Chapter Four

Where Self-Esteem and Your Future Begin

In my previous books, and often from stage, speaking, I've had the task of defining, in the simplest possible terms, how programming works, and where our self-identities begin. Here is my most concise summary:

From the moment you were born, every message you received was recorded in your brain. Everything you heard, everything you saw, everything you thought, everything you said, everything you experienced, was recorded in your brain—temporarily.

Then, every message you received that was *repeated* often enough was wired into your brain 'permanently' as a new program in your operating system. The result is that the programs you have received—about anything––have been wired into your brain, and those programs determine what you believe—about anything—today.

It doesn't make any difference if the programs you received were 'true' or not. The part of the brain that stores those programs doesn't know the difference between something that's true and something that's false.

Your brain just stores the programs it gets—and it acts on those programs as though they're *true*. (This is why so many people can be so wrong about so many things, and still believe they're right; their brains are *wired* to believe they're right.)

The 148,000 *No's*

It has been estimated that during the first 18 years of life, the average person, growing up in a reasonably positive home, is told *'no,'* or what he or she *'cannot'* do, more than 148,000 times!

During the first 18 years of *your* life, how many times were you told how *exceptional* you are, what you *can* do, or what you *could* become?

Even if you were fortunate, with parents or role models who showed you your true potential, it is likely that the thousands of *no's* you received from the world around you far outweighed the *yes's* you received during the same time.

The result of that kind of programming is that we end up where we are today, with our brains improperly wired, or often wired to work *against* us.

The Newborn Nursery

Most of us have had the opportunity to visit a hospital's newborn nursery, where we first look in on precious little infants just after they're born. In the nursery, we usually observe the infants through a viewing window. There, on the other side of the window, snuggled in their little bassinets, we see those remarkable miracles of life.

Imagine looking in on a couple of those infants right now. They are amazing! If they're awake, and their eyes are open, we can see them looking out at their world for the first time, as though they're searching, waiting for that incredible life they were born to live.

When we look into the eyes of those infants, what we see is *unlimited opportunity and endless possibility*. They have their entire lives in front of them. Their potential is infinite.

It's clear that each of those infants was born to succeed! (*No one* is *ever* born to fail.) In fact, everything about those little infants is designed to help each of them reach their greatest potential and live a life that fulfills their highest promise. That's what they were born to do!

But then, even as they leave the warm, comfortable security of their birthing bassinet, and after a short stay in a hospital room, the first moments of the infant's programming has already begun. From the mother's first words, to the television screen in the corner of the room, messages are feeding into that child's brain.

Soon, mother, father, brothers, sisters, other family members, and in time, friends, teachers, media, the internet, and every other programming source in that young person's life join in with message after message—countless, tens of thousands of messages—and the child's brain is designed to take it all in. (It's called 'learning.')

As the child continues to grow, in their brain, whatever they hear often enough is forming the picture of who that child believes himself or herself to be, and what is 'true' about anything. Almost everything they think is being formed by the repetition of programs they receive.

It doesn't make any difference if the programs they receive are actually true or not. With enough repetition, *any* program can become *truth* in the child's brain.

As an example, instead of being born, brought home, and raised as you were, in the home you grew up in, imagine that you had been kidnapped as an infant and taken to a different home, brought up in a different country, and raised by different parents in a completely different part of the world.

Instead of being 'you,' with the name, and the family and the friends and the education and the experience and the beliefs you now have, you would be the product of an entirely different environment. You would still be 'you' genetically—but everything else about 'you' would be different. Your beliefs about almost everything—your faith, your ideology, your habits, the way you dress, your attitudes, your work, your relationships, your goals, your future—virtually everything about you would be different.

In fact, if that had actually happened, you could even view the person you are in your real life today as an enemy—and you could think and believe the *opposite* of almost everything you think and believe today.

We are all born to excel—to live up to our greatest promise, with our whole lives in front of us. But then, all too often, something happens that interrupts that process—and it can change everything. Not as dramatic as being stolen from our crib, perhaps, but something happens to us that *does* redirect, and often changes, the course of the rest of our life.

The programs we receive end up forming what we believe, and what we think about everything. Our programs tell us who we are, and even what we will—or will *not* do—every day of our lives.

The Results

Take a moment, right now, while you're reading this, and think of someone you know, or know of, whom you would consider to be a truly successful person.

I don't mean just financially successful, but successful in *life*. This would be someone whose self-esteem is high, someone whose life is working! Someone who is living a life that is fulfilled, and always moving upwards. It would probably be someone you would like to spend time with, or emulate and learn from.

Your picture could be of someone who is living now, or someone who isn't. But whoever it is, get a picture of that most successful person in your mind now, so you can see them clearly.

While you're holding a picture of that wonderfully successful person in your mind, I'd like you to imagine that she or he is actually there with you right now. In your mind's eye, imagine that the person is standing not too far from you, off to the right of you. And for the moment, we'll just ask that person to stand there.

Then, with the successful person waiting there, calmly and patiently, we're going to add someone else to our experiment.

To do this, I would like you now to think of someone you would see as being *unsuccessful.* This would be someone you know, or know of, who is literally *failing* at life.

When I think of the least successful person I know, I see the picture of a young kid who left home because of drug use when he was seventeen years old, and his parents have never seen him since. If they did find him now, years later, they would probably find him in an alley somewhere, and it's possible he wouldn't even recognize his own parents because of the amount of drugs or chemicals in his system.

That's the person who comes to my mind when I think of someone who is 'failing' in every way. But in your own mind, think of an example of someone you know, or know of, who fits your picture of failure. Whoever it is, get a clear image of that person in your mind.

Then, for the moment, imagine that person is also there with you right now, and is standing off to the left of you.

Now, in this experiment, you should have two people standing near you. Off to your right is the person who is *succeeding* in life. On your left is the person who is *failing* in life.

Take a moment and examine each of them. Get a good picture of them in your mind.

One of them—the successful one on the right—is living a life that works. Successful in every important way. Uplifting and fulfilling. Happy and feeling good about life.

The other person—the unsuccessful one on the left—has self-esteem of such a low level that it has affected everything about them. This person is failing and spiraling downward. Unhappy and living a life that is not working.

This next question holds one of the most important answers you can ever know:

Question: What is the real *difference* between the two people? What is the difference between the person whose life is *working* and the person whose life is *not working*?

Answer: The difference between the two people is their *programs*.

It is their programs, given to them after they were born, that caused them to live their lives in different ways. Those programs created the success or failure each of them has now.

They Both Had Unlimited Potential

What makes this picture even more profound is that those two people could have been the two infants we saw in the newborn nursery, just a short time ago! When we looked in on them in the nursery, each of them, with their eyes wide open, were searching, waiting to live out the unlimited potential they were each born to achieve!

And now, after time has passed, and their brains were wired, and the programs took hold, here they are, *completely different* in the outcome of their lives!

That difference reveals one of the most important truths we can ever learn about human behavior, and even about life itself.

When those two people were infants, the potential to live a complete and fulfilling life was the same for each of them. But one of them ended up being wired to *succeed*. The other one ended up being wired to *fail*.

People who argue against this would tell you that it was just life's challenges, its ups and downs, that got in the way and changed the infant who failed. And they would say that it was good luck or fortune that interceded and made the successful person successful. Or they might say that it was just the difference in the two individuals' DNA.

But that's not the answer. The person who receives better, healthier, more *positive* programs will, over time, virtually always do better than the person who receives unhealthy, *negative* programs.

If you know someone who is doing really well, year after year, and continues to do so in spite of life's challenges—that's *programs;* that is how their brain is wired.

If you know someone who is failing, time after time, and continues to fail, and even with help can't seem to get life right—that, too, is *programs;* that is how *their* brain is wired.

What Are Your Programs Now?

As you probably guessed from the above picture, it's clear that when you're dealing with self-esteem, you should start by looking at your own programs—and begin to recognize any programs you have now that could be creating the wrong image of you.

If any of your self-talk tells you are less than you should be, it will create programs that pull you down to that level—and you will have to change those programs if you want your self-esteem to be whole again.

Choose to wire your own brain with the right, positive programs of strong self-esteem—the messages that should have been given to you in the first place. And forever, get rid of the self-talk that's negative or works against you.

Chapter Five

Negative Self-Talk, Low Self-Esteem

Most of us can understand that when we were growing up, we got programmed, and we end up living out the programs we got—whether they were good programs or bad.

Negative Self-Talk

The ultimate creator of low self-esteem is negative self-talk. And it is because of programming that we have so much of it. In its simplest form, negative self-talk is easy to spot. It sounds like this:

"Nothing ever goes right for me."

"I'm nobody."

"I look terrible."

"I'm just not good enough."

"Who would ever listen to me?"

"That's impossible!"

"Why even try?"

"I can't do anything right."

"Leave it to me, I'll mess it up."

"I'm just not attractive."

"There's just no way."

"I can't handle this."

"I just know it won't work."

"That's easy for you to say."

"I can't stand to look at myself in the mirror."

"I'm just not up to it."

"I never reach the goals I set."

"There's nothing I can do."

"Life sucks!"

"Today just isn't my day."

"Born to lose."

Every one of those messages is negative. And every one of them is harmful.

Can you imagine repeatedly typing directions like those into your mental computer—especially if your brain is going to accept them as truth? *We do it all the time!* And the more you say them or think them, the more *wired-in* and *true* those directions become!

Negative self-talk goes far beyond those few, small examples, of course. It enters into and influences virtually every area of our lives. Here are a few more examples. Have you ever said anything like any of the following? Read through this list and see if you find yourself in any of them:

"The only luck I have is bad luck."

"I'm so clumsy!"

"I'm so stupid."

"I'm too shy."

"I never know what to say."

"I never win at anything."

"I just wasn't cut out for that."

"I don't have the energy."

"Nobody likes me."

"I never make enough money."

"Everything I touch turns to bleep."

"I can never get ahead."

"Nobody listens to me."

"I never know what to do."

"I'm no good at math."

"I'm just not creative."

"I just wasn't cut out for that."

"I can never lose weight."

"Everything I eat goes right to my waist."

"My kids are driving me crazy."

"This will be the death of me."

"I can never seem to get organized."

"I already know I won't like it."

"I never have enough time."

"I don't have the patience for that."

"I never have enough money left over at the end of the month."

"Sometimes I just hate myself!"

"I'm not up to it."

"When will I ever learn?"

"Why even try?"

"I wish I'd never been born."

"It's just no use."

Those few examples give just a slight hint of the kind of language that directs millions of lives toward destructive self-esteem.

When you even *think* those self-talk messages, or thousands of others just like them, even when they pass unnoticed through your mind, <u>*you are wiring your brain to make them true. You are wiring your brain to fail*</u>.

No one *tries* to do that to themselves, of course. When you use negative self-talk, you're just repeating the messages that have been previously wired into your brain. But once you know how it works, it's time to do something about it.

If, in the past, it seemed as though your brain was working against you, there is light ahead. Your brain is designed to help you, not hurt you. Let's see how it works.

Chapter Six

Self-Esteem, Self-Talk, and Your Brain

Although the process by which self-talk rewires your brain is somewhat complicated, this overview will simplify the process.

The Neuroplasticity of Your Brain

Neuroplasticity refers to your brain's ability to form new neural networks and connections based on new input. This process takes place throughout your lifetime.

This means that your brain is always learning, and it is always changing. New learning or experience actually changes the physical structure—the wiring—of your brain.

Research into the brain's neuroplasticity has opened new doors of treatment for stroke victims, as well as for people who struggle with dyslexia, learning disorders, and even brain damage.

The key here is that research in the field of neuroscience has identified the link between your thoughts and how your brain is wired. What you experience, what you think, and what you say changes the synaptic connections in your brain.

This means that what you have been thinking and saying—without being aware of it—has been wiring and changing your brain.

Your Brain Believes What It is Told Most

Deep inside the workings of the human brain, there is no actual '*truth*.' The part of the brain that stores all of the messages you have received accepts what it is told most often—and those become the strongest messages. The brain then plays those messages back to you, and as I noted earlier, it presents them to you as 'truth' or 'fact,' whether the messages are actually true or not.

That's why you can believe in one political ideology completely, when the other half of the population—many millions of people—believes in the opposite political ideology. And you, and all of them, each think your own beliefs are correct. (A perfect example of this is that many people, when voting, are actually voting based on the programmed biases that have been wired, through repetition, into their brains—not on the actual qualifications of the candidate.)

Are Your Programs Helping You or Hurting You?

What you believe about anything is not a measure of its correctness. What you believe about anything is a measure of the programs you have that support your belief.

This is also true of your self-esteem. Your brain has stored an immense number of programs about *you*—everything you believe to be true about you.

If enough of your programs are negative, your self-talk will also be negative. This is because your present self-talk is the result of the programs you have that are the strongest. The rule is: Negative programs equal negative self-talk.

And it is in negative and inaccurate programs that low self-esteem lives.

Neuroplasticity and *Repetition*

You'll notice that occasionally, throughout this book, I have made it a point to repeat certain points of information that are especially important. There is a reason for the repetition.

Reading something more than once, or several times, helps to ensure that the brain will wire the information into its long-term memory. Repetition creates retention.

It is also repetition that plays the greatest role in wiring your brain to create positive self-esteem—or negative self-esteem. Because of the brain's neuroplasticity, the most important key to wiring or rewiring your brain is repetition. The brain is designed to pay attention to, and store, the messages that are repeated most often.

As I have often said, the key to success is repetition. *Repetition, repetition, repetition.*

A message your brain receives only once will be stored in your brain's short-term memory only briefly. It doesn't become 'wired in' to your brain's long-term storage files. But when that same message is repeated frequently, your brain begins to form new neural connections. It wires the new message into, and connects it with, the vast neural networks of your conscious and unconscious mind.

It is because your brain stores messages that are repeated that *you end up believing the things about you that you tell yourself most*. The complete 'you' that you believe you are today is the combined result of years of messages you have received from the world around you, and—most importantly—the repeated messages you have been giving to yourself through your own self-talk.

This means that whatever messages you got from others, combined with what your experiences have caused you to say to yourself in your own self-talk, have created everything you believe to be true about yourself today.

Some of the messages your brain received about you may have been true. But many of the messages your brain received and wired in were not true at all!

Together, those inaccurate messages, through lifelong repetition, have created every negative belief you have about yourself. Your self-doubts, your imagined inadequacies, most of your fears, and everything you believe incorrectly about who you are today, are the result of the repetition of messages to your brain.

If the programming of the brain is based on repetition, and if your own self-talk is negative, and tells you that you're not good enough, or that you don't measure up, what is the only outcome you can predict?

The only outcome you can predict is self-esteem that gives you a false and limited picture of yourself.

As we've learned, we continually—and unconsciously—repeat and replay the programs that are the strongest. This is incredibly important because, in the brain, the strongest programs always win.

The solution to most problems of negative self-esteem is clear—we need to rewire our brains with something more 'positive.'

But isn't positive thinking nothing more than 'wishful' thinking? Let's take a look.

Your Prefrontal Cortex

At one time, skeptics believed that "positive thinking" was nothing more than wishful thinking, and that the idea of positive thinking was something you could read about in a self-help book—but it wouldn't really make your life any better. Subsequent brain research, however, has shown an entirely different story.

People who have trained their brains to think in the *positive,* wire more neural networks into the *left* prefrontal cortex of their brain. (Reach up and tap the area just above your left eyebrow.) That's a part of the brain that helps you seek options and alternatives, helps you find better ways to deal with problems, boosts your attitude, and puts you into positive action.

Obviously, having good, strong wiring in your *left* prefrontal cortex is very important. *Positive* self-talk strengthens—wires more connections into—that part of your brain.

And what about *negative* self-talkers?

People who habitually think in the *negative* wire more neural networks into the *right* prefrontal cortex of their brains. (Now tap just above your right eyebrow.) That's a part of the brain that causes you to *shut down your options,* makes you feel down or depressed, puts you into escape mode, and stops you from solving the problem or taking action.

(If you tapped your forehead just now, did you automatically think of yourself as having a stronger *left* prefrontal cortex, or a stronger *right* prefrontal cortex? That is, do you see yourself as more of a positive thinker, or as someone who has more negative thoughts?)

Today, breakthroughs in neuroscience that tell us why self-talk is a major player in our behavior—and our individual well-being in life—have become commonplace. Neuroscience has identified the importance of positive attitudes and even where they reside in the brain. The takeaway from our current understanding of brain physiology makes it clear that our thoughts not only become wired into our brain—they change the *structure* of the brain itself.

* * *

Self-Talk and Your Subconscious Mind

Your subconscious mind makes most of your choices for you—without your being aware of it.

That's kind of scary when you recognize that as much as 90% or more of your mental programs are buried in your subconscious mind—*and are completely hidden from you!* It is safe to say that you have virtually tens of thousands of programs that are directing your life right now, and you are not actually aware of what most of those programs are.

It has been estimated that, in the average individual, 77% or more of their unconscious programs are *negative* and may be working against them.

This means that not only is your subconscious mind silently making most of your choices for you, but it is also making those choices based on programs that are mostly *negative.*

Your thoughts—thousands of them each day—are controlled by the programs you have spent years storing in your subconscious mind.

If, by mistake, you programmed the navigational computer on an airplane to fly north, when you wanted to fly south, the airplane will follow its computer program and fly north—*even if it's not where you want to go.*

If you program the directional computer of your own brain to send you in the wrong direction, that is the direction your thoughts and your actions will take you—even if it's not where you want to go.

The obvious solution to this problem would be to get rid of the mental programs you have that are negative, and to make sure you have enough positive programs stored in your subconscious mind to ensure that your attitudes and actions will also be positive.

But the dilemma has been: How do you get rid of negative programs when they are hidden—when they are buried deep in your subconscious mind—and you don't even know what they are? How do you fix the problem of negative self-talk, and the mass of negative programs it creates?

'Pruning' Out Bad Programs

The answer lies in an activity of the brain neuroscientists refer to as '*pruning*.'

Because there is a limit to the brain's capacity to store information (it only has so much space), it has to get rid of information it no longer uses—to make room for new information that might be important.

<u>Your brain is designed to *delete* the programs it no longer uses</u>. When you give new, repeated messages to your brain, those messages become wired in. If they're strong messages, the brain will begin to replace the old messages with the new.

This means that when you begin wiring in positive new messages—and stop wiring your brain with negative messages—your brain will prune out—delete—the old, negative messages that were literally wiring your self-esteem with the wrong information.

* * *

To learn which messages you need to begin giving to your brain—especially those that will build your self-esteem—let's now take a look at your level of self-esteem as it is today.

Chapter Seven

The Self-Esteem Quiz

You are a wonderfully complex individual. How you feel about yourself is not made up of one or two simple measures; it is made up of your evaluation of yourself in many important areas of your life. I've identified fifteen of these areas for you here:

Your Personal Appearance

How you think and feel about how you look, plays an important role in how you see yourself as an individual. To some extent, personal appearance is a factor in almost everyone's self-esteem.

Your Intelligence

To some people, their personal intelligence defines them as an individual, and it plays a leading role in forming their self-esteem.

Your Relationships

How well you see yourself relating to others can be important in several ways: in intimate relationships; how well you get along in groups; the degree to which you see yourself as a leader or a follower, and how you deal with people one-on-one.

Your Attitude

The importance of your attitude cannot be overstated. It plays a vital role in how you view yourself, the world you live in, and what you do about it each day. *'Great,' 'average,'* or *'down,'* your attitude affects your self-esteem, and your self-esteem affects your attitude.

Your Health and Fitness

How you feel about your health, and how you view its importance to you, will determine what you do about it—which is part of how you treat yourself—which is a direct result of how you feel about yourself.

Your Money and Finances

Financial well-being almost always follows financial identity; you will strive to only acquire what you see yourself as worth having.

Your Energy and Vitality

Your enthusiasm, and the vitality you present to the world each day are, in part, governed by how you view yourself—alive, strong, interested, and energetic, or weak, hesitant, and unsure.

Your Integrity & Honesty

Your self-esteem defines your strength of character, and your insistence on living up to it. The amount of integrity and honesty you exhibit is the result of their importance to you, and your level of self-worth.

Your Courage and Will

Courage and will are born of inner strength––and inner strength is born of self-esteem. The greater your estimation of yourself, the more courage and will you have on your side.

Your Spirituality

This area refers not so much to religious beliefs, but rather to the level of your conviction that there is something greater than your '*self*,' and your personal relationship with a higher meaning in your life.

Your Purpose

Some people define their entire lives by a sense of purpose that drives them, energizes them, and spurs them on. People with low self-esteem often have trouble accepting a clear purpose in their lives, because they have not yet accepted themselves as being significant enough to have one.

Your Discipline

How you view your success in managing your life, dealing with opportunities, issues and demands, and getting things done.

Your Achievement

How you view the value of your achievements is a reflection of the value you place on yourself achieving them. Strong self-esteem fosters a positive pride in accomplishment. Diminished self-esteem sees achievements as temporary, accidental, or undeserved.

Your Personal Potential

How you view your future potential is a property of how you view yourself. Your estimation of your potential as an individual is a direct reflection of your belief in yourself—which is a direct result of your self-esteem.

Your Overall Quality as an Individual

How you see yourself as successfully living up to the measure of the person you were born to be.

* * *

There are additional areas you could explore when you're evaluating your self-esteem, of course. These would include your *direction, commitment, effort, compassion, charity, trust, manners, humility, patience, mindfulness,* and *optimism,* among others. However, the fifteen areas we're focusing on here will give you a good picture of key areas in your life in which you are either building your self-esteem or holding yourself back.

* * *

In the following quiz, you will have the opportunity to rate yourself in each of the fifteen areas. Take your time with your evaluation. No one is going to grade you, but you're going to be grading yourself.

(I have made a printable PDF of this quiz available for you to download. I recommend you print out several copies, so you can continue to update your scores and your progress going forward. To download *The Self-Esteem Quiz,* go to www.selftalkplus.com/selfesteemquiz.)

The Self-Esteem Quiz

Rate how you feel about yourself from *1* to *10* in each of the areas below. (*1* is low, *10* is high.)

1. ☐ **Your Personal Appearance**

How you think you look, and how you feel about how you look.

2. ☐ **Your Intelligence**

How smart you believe you are, and how important your intelligence is to you.

3. ☐ **Your Relationships**

How well you see yourself relating to others.

4. ☐ **Your Attitude**

How you typically view life as you go through the day.

5. ☐ **Your Health and Fitness**

How you feel about your health and fitness, and how you view their importance to you.

6. ☐ Your Money and Finances

How you feel about money, your financial status, and the level of financial wealth you feel you deserve.

7. ☐ Your Energy and Vitality

How 'alive' and interested you are.

8. ☐ Your Integrity & Honesty

How you feel about your honesty.

9. ☐ Your Courage and Will

How you feel about your personal inner strength.

10. ☐ Your Spirituality

The role spirituality plays in your life, and how you see yourself as a spiritual person.

11. ☐ Your Purpose

How you feel about having a purpose in life, and whether or not you have identified yours.

12. ☐ Your Discipline

How you feel about taking the necessary action to deal with life's opportunities and demands.

13. ☐ Your Achievement

How you feel about your level of accomplishment.

14. ☐ Your Personal Potential

How you feel about future achievements, and how you view the opportunity, overall, you have for being successful.

15. ☐ Your Overall Quality as an Individual

How you rate yourself in terms of living up to the best of who you were born to be.

a. **What are your three highest scores?**

____

b. **What are your three lowest scores?**

____

c. **What is your total, overall score?**

____

d. **What would you like your overall score to be six months from today?**

__________ Today's date: __________

* * *

How did you do? Were any of your scores lower than you'd like them to be?

As you begin to work on raising your scores, you'll find that when you improve your score in even one or two of the areas, other scores will also, automatically, start to improve, even if you're not focusing on them directly. That's because when you switch your self-talk from negative to positive, you're changing your outlook not just in one or two areas—you're reinventing how you look at life.

I recommend that you print out the quiz and take it again in 90 days, and again in six months. If you don't download and print out the quiz, be sure to write down your scores, so you can measure your progress.

Now let's look at the kind of self-talk that will help you improve your scores.

Chapter Eight

Changing Your Self-Talk—Changing Your Self-Esteem

Earlier, we looked at examples of self-talk of the negative kind. Since the goal is to begin to turn *all* of your self-talk into the healthiest, most positive kind, we'll start by examining some of the old, negative self-talk messages, and turning them around. In its simplest form, it begins like this:

Instead of saying, *"Nothing ever goes right for me,"* you would now say,

"Things usually work out well for me."

Instead of saying, *"I'm nobody,"* you would say,

"I'm somebody. I'm me, and I count."

Instead of saying, *"I'm not good enough,"* you would replace it with,

"I've got this! I can do it, and I'll prove it!"

Instead of saying, *"Who would ever listen to me?"* you would now say,

"I have a good mind, and it shows. When I talk, people listen."

Instead of saying, *"I can't stand to look at myself in the mirror,"* you would immediately replace it with,

"I like who I see when I look in the mirror. I'm my best friend, and I always let myself know how well I'm doing."

When people start to change their self-talk in this way, one of the first things that comes to their mind is that it sounds too positive, or that they're not being truthful with themselves. But the real truth is, it is their old, *negative* self-talk that hasn't been truthful—it's been lying to them for *years!* Their new self-talk is finally getting it *right!*

When you start listening to the right self-talk, or start rephrasing it like we are here, it will feel strange at first—but that's just your old programs telling you they don't want to let go; they want you to stay just like you were.

Ignore them. In time, if you stay with it, the old programs will fall into disuse, your brain will prune them out, and they will become a thing of the past. They were bad programs, they were wrong, and you don't need them any longer.

Here are more examples of what the right self-talk sounds like:

Instead of saying, *"I can't handle this,"* you would immediately stop yourself and say,

"I'm fine, I'm doing great! I'm on top, in tune, in touch, and going for it!"

Instead of ever again saying, *"Today just isn't my day,"* you would turn it around and say,

"Today is my day. Just watch me, and I'll prove it!"

Instead of saying, *"I wish I'd never been born,"* you would now say,

"I am glad to be alive, and so glad to be here—today especially!"

Instead of even *thinking* the thought, *"I just can't win,"* you would replace it with,

"I'm a great learner. I love every chance I have to learn—and learning is winning."

Those kinds of reframed thoughts aren't simplistic platitudes—they're new *directions* to your brain. Your brain takes them seriously, and so should you.

Replacing *"I'm not good enough,"* with *"I can do this,"* may sound so simple that it couldn't possibly make a real difference in your life—but don't let yourself be put off by the apparent simplicity of the change in your self-talk. Because of neuroplasticity, what's taking place in your brain is profound.

What is Your Story?

Each of us has a story. Some people repeat their story so often, everyone around them knows the story by heart. Other people are quieter about their stories; but they still repeat them in their own minds.

A short look at a part of the story told by someone who has low self-esteem might sound like this:

"I don't think I've ever had a lucky day in my life. It must have been raining the day I was born. Maybe that's why I have so many problems. I had a tough childhood and I never got any breaks. I still

don't. It seems like the world is out to get me. I keep waiting for my luck to change, but it just doesn't happen. I had a shot at getting hired in a good job, but I guess it just wasn't my lucky day. That seems to be the way it always goes for me. A day late and a dollar short. I'm living alone again, and right now I'm just hanging on. I'm not sure what I'm going to do."

Now, giving us a very different take on life, here is a brief look at the story of someone who has practiced creating positive self-esteem:

"What an incredible day! I'm glad to be here and going for it. My life hasn't always been easy, but that's how you learn. I must have been born with a smile on my face. I'm not where I want to be yet, but I'm working at it, and I'm doing it. My life is full of opportunities, so I'm careful to choose the ones I want. I'm a goal-setter, so I've got a good idea where I'm going and what it's going to take to get there. And getting there is half the fun. I don't mind problems. I wouldn't be alive if I didn't have a few challenges. They just make you stronger."

Those are just short excerpts of people's broader stories—the same kinds of expressions we hear from people all the time. They're important because stories like those not only define who the person is; they set the direction in that person's life *for more of the same*.

When other people hear *your* personal story, what does it sound like? Is your story filled with pictures of you being a victim and fraught with problems, struggling through an endless list of difficulties? Or, when you tell your story, does it have a sense of optimism, with pictures of positive experiences, overcoming the obstacles with hard work, hope and promise?

The next time you hear yourself telling your story, see what happens when you change the old language that centers on difficulty and failure, and replace it with the new language that centers on gratitude and possibility. When you do, you change the story of what is yet to come.

Learning the New Language

We've looked at turning negative self-talk around, so it works for you instead of against you. But because self-esteem is a subject that deals with many areas of your life, fixing it asks you to do more than just correcting a few words now and then.

Here is an actual self-talk learning script on the subject of self-esteem, transcribed from an audio session on the Institute's listening website. Reading through these passages carefully, you can see how combining a variety of messages together, creates an entire 'environment of thinking' about the subject.

From the self-talk program:
"Positive Self-Talk for Self-Esteem"
(Session 2)

I know that self-esteem is the picture of me that I hold of myself in my mind.

I recognize that self-esteem is built word by word, thought by thought, and action by action.

I know that the building of true, life-long self-esteem is always up to the individual.

I believe that building my own self-esteem, and creating more of it, is always my responsibility.

I enjoy taking responsibility for the way I feel about myself.

Building self-esteem makes me feel better about myself, and it always makes my life better in every imaginable way.

I know that my appreciation of others, and of everything around me, is a direct result of my appreciation for myself. I believe in appreciating who I am.

I know that I create my own self-esteem with every thought that I think about myself, and with every picture that I create in my mind.

Creating self-esteem is never difficult for me.

Creating self-esteem is a positive habit, and a way of life.

I believe that positive self-esteem is essential to a life well-lived. Living a good life starts with having strong self-esteem.

I recognize that no one else can ever play any role in reducing my self-esteem, or taking it from me.

I know that I alone am in control of who I am and what I believe about myself.

I understand that my self-esteem is made up of the programs of myself that I carry in my mind. And I know that building the best of those programs is always up to me.

I know that good self-esteem is never an accident. And I know that good self-esteem is always a matter of choice.

I believe that the quality of life is always a reflection of the self-esteem that I create for myself.

The greater, and more positive, my self-esteem, the greater, and more positive, is the quality of my life.

I know that even the most negative programs of self-esteem I may have received in the past can be replaced with new programs of self-esteem that I choose for myself. And because I understand this, I always choose the programs that are the best.

Replacing old programs with new programs is fun and easy for me.

I really like knowing that I can create the best possible picture of me in my mind. I like knowing it, I like doing it, and I like living it!

* * *

Imagine wiring your brain with those kinds of messages every day. Keeping in mind that the brain acts on the strongest programs it receives, imagine what those kinds of programs could do for you and your future!

A few pages of positive self-talk in a book aren't intended to suddenly remake your self-esteem in two or three minutes, of course. But, enough of the right self-talk, combined with the continuing force of daily repetition, will override the earlier program circuits in your brain—and replace them.

<u>The more your brain receives the new messages, the more those messages will become permanently wired in, and the more the old, negative messages will be pruned out of your life and erased for good.</u>

What Critics Might Say

After reading only a few examples of self-talk, like those in this book, people who don't understand self-talk or what's behind it, might say that the self-talk only focuses on the 'good,' so they believe it's unrealistic.

But the right kind of self-talk isn't like that at all. Correctly-worded self-talk confronts problems head on and deals with them directly—and forcefully! It never ignores problems or difficulties; it recognizes them and helps you deal with them one by one—and take action!

People who learn self-talk by listening to it have said that learning the right self-talk is like going through a mental boot camp for fifteen minutes every morning—very positive and helpful, but a serious workout for the brain. (To hear a good example of this, check out the program entitled *Taking Control of Your Life* on the Institute's website www.selftalkplus.com).

Not everyone understands positive self-talk, of course, no matter how practical it is. As an example of this, one man expressed that it was 'wrong' to try to see the world in a positive way, that life was filled with mostly problems and difficulties, and that to try to see it differently was putting your head in the sand.

I felt bad for that individual. He could not see that he was speaking only from his own programs of despair; he was thinking from the wrong prefrontal cortex of his brain—the negative part—and he didn't understand that his own programs were putting his head not in the sand, but in a vise that did not want to let him go.

Low self-esteem often tries to do that. Made up of programs of defeat and despair, negative self-esteem can cause the suffering person to defend their right to see the world only as dark and difficult, and set against them, and they will argue endlessly to prove they are right. To them, the glass is always half empty, and they fight for the right to see it that way. It's not really true, of course, but that's what negative programs do.

Fortunately, even if you feel the world is a dark place to live, or that you can't measure up, it does not take a miracle to rise above the doubts and fear. It takes only your desire to get better, and the willingness to look for that one ray of light that tells you there is hope. I believe that ray of light is found in positive self-talk.

The Goal is to Begin

The goal isn't to become the confident, thoughtful, responsible, positive self-talking person overnight. The goal is to *begin*—to start here, now, wherever you are today. Decide what you want the outcome to be. Start with one determined day of positive self-talk. And then another. And then another.

The solution is to learn a new language—the language of positive self-talk—and *really* learn it. Learn the new language so well that you

begin to speak it naturally, day in and day out, without having to think about it. When you do, your *self-esteem* will be learning—and growing–
–right along with you.

Chapter Nine

The Next Steps

Now we come to the critical and very exciting moment in the goal to change our self-esteem. It is the moment when we have the necessary facts assembled, and are faced with the potentially life-changing choice to take action and make the change.

The facts we have so far are these:

a. Your self-esteem is formed by a lifetime of programs you received, first from others, and then from the programs you received from yourself, through your own self-talk.

b. The key to wiring programs into the brain is repetition. The more the message is repeated, the stronger your brain wires it in.

c. The part of the brain that stores its programs doesn't know the difference between a program that is true and a program that is false.

d. The brain acts on the programs it has that are the strongest.

e. Repeated *negative* self-talk creates *negative* self-esteem programs in the brain.

f. Repeated *positive* self-talk creates *positive* self-esteem programs in the brain.

g. Negative programs in the brain can be replaced and erased by the repetition of new positive programs.

h. The new language created by the repetition of positive self-talk forms the foundation for long-term, positive self-esteem.

With what we have learned about the human brain, and how faulty or inaccurate messaging creates low self-esteem, we now know what to do about it.

For the many years I have been studying this subject, my primary goal has been to educate people on how the process works, and also to help people change their self-esteem in the easiest and the most practical ways possible.

Here's a summary of what I have found.

Changing Your Self-Talk

In previous books, I've included the *Guide to Changing Your Self-Talk* from the Self-Talk Institute. This guide is based on more than thirty-five years of research and experience in teaching self-talk methods and techniques, and it is very effective. I'll outline their recommendations for you here.

According to the Institute's guide, the key steps to changing your self-talk are:

1. **Monitor**
2. **Edit**
3. **Listen**
4. **Practice**

1. Monitor

Monitor means to listen to your *current* self-talk. To get into the habit of doing this, practice monitoring everything you *say,* and everything you *think,* for a minimum of the next 30 days.

That's something anyone can do, but it can take some effort. Most of us aren't in the habit of examining every thought we have, or being consciously aware of reflecting on everything we say. When you practice paying attention to everything you think or say for a month, you learn *exactly* what self-talk—good or bad—is in control in your life right now.

When you monitor your current self-talk, pay special attention to any self-talk you've been using up to now that describes you, or how you feel about you, or defines you in any way. That's the self-talk that is most directly setting up your self-esteem.

2. Edit

Edit means to immediately begin changing your conscious self-talk from bad to good. Edit anything you're about to say that is negative, harmful, or could work against you. Replace it with new, on-the-spot, positive self-talk that will help you—especially self-talk that defines you in a healthy, more positive way.

Everyone, with a little effort, has the ability to stop anything they were about to think or say that is negative, turn it around, and think or say the opposite—something that helps instead of hurts.

Editing, by itself, won't get rid of the old programs you already have that are stored in your brain that have been pulling you down—but it will keep you from getting any more like them.

3. Listen

Listen means to listen to recorded sessions of self-talk. Learning self-talk by listening to it gives you the repetition necessary to wire the new messages into your brain. Doing this uses the same techniques that are used to learn a new language by listening to it.

Listening to self-talk replaces and erases the old negative programs you have stored. (As you listen, the new programs will be wired in, and the brain will begin to prune out the old programs.)

When people listen to self-talk, they have a choice in how their self-talk comes to them. The sessions are either downloaded permanently to their computers from the Self-Talk Institute's online store (www.selftalkstore.com), or they're streamed directly to the users' phones or listening devices (www.selftalkplus.com).

In the second option—when the users stream self-talk sessions to their listening devices—they have unlimited access to all of the Institute's complete catalog of self-talk listening programs at no cost for a period of thirty days.

This allows even the most hardened skeptic to listen to self-talk as often as they want, every day for a month, and begin learning the new self-talk for themselves. (The Institute also makes self-talk sessions available at no cost to anyone who wants to listen but feels they can't afford it—so there's *no* reason not to listen.)

4. Practice

Practice means to consciously work at monitoring and editing your self-talk, and practice changing and replacing—without exception—any self-talk that works against you in any way.

Practicing works best when you're actively looking for the opportunities each day to change your self-talk—including your thoughts—to create a different frame of mind. Most days will give you many of those opportunities.

Note: It may have taken years to gather the programs you now have—but it doesn't take years to delete them. When you're working at rewiring your brain, neuroplasticity is working for you. (Remember, your brain wants to get rid of old programs it is no longer using. When you wire in new programs, they will replace the old programs, and the old circuitry will be pruned out.)

It takes about three weeks or more for the brain to *begin* to wire in the new messages.

When you set a goal to change your self-talk and your self-esteem, plan to stay with it long enough to give your brain the necessary time for the new wiring to take place. And then, keep doing it. The more you do, the stronger the new programs will become.

Then, when you've successfully begun to replace the old, negative programs in two or three areas, you can start doing the same in additional areas that you also want to improve.

The New Programs Become the Real You

Because it is repetition itself that wires the new messages into your brain, the more you listen to, or practice, positive self-talk, the more natural it becomes.

Usually, within a few days, you'll begin to automatically correct yourself anytime some of the old, negative self-talk crops up. Within even a few weeks, you should find that your picture of yourself is actually changing. That means the repetition is working, and you're beginning to imprint the new messages of self-esteem into your brain.

Chapter Ten

You Can Do This!

If you'd like to have better self-esteem, there is clearly something you can do about it. However you decide to change your self-talk and rewire your brain with a more accurate, more positive picture of you, I encourage you to do it. Go for it! You might as well. You were born to excel, and it's time to see the real you!

It's been my experience that many people who suffer low self-esteem allow it to go on because they believe there is nothing they can do about it; that's just life, and they believe they have to accept what life sends them.

But it isn't 'just life,' and you don't have to accept it. You have the right to see yourself as you choose, and your self-esteem is up to you.

You also have the right to experience the joy of getting to know the very best you—as you really are. You have the right to feel good about yourself, and know that you're a person of quality—the *highest* quality.

Beginning now, you get to create the picture of you that you would most like to see. When you do, you won't be kidding yourself; you'll be revealing the remarkable, valuable, quality person you really are.

As you take this next step in your journey upward, I wish you my heartfelt, very best! You deserve it in so many ways.

Shad Helmstetter, Ph.D.
June, 2020

Tools and ResourcesYou Can Use:

Listening to Self-Talk
www.selftalkplus.com

Self-Talk Trainer Certification
www.selftalkinstitute.com

Life Coach Training and Certification
www.lifecoachinstitute.com

To contact Shad Helmstetter
Email: shadhelmstetteroffice@gmail.com

Printed in Great Britain
by Amazon

19062719R00058